WILD WICKED WONDERFUL

TOP 10:

PARTNERSHIPS

By Virginia Loh-Hagan

45th Parallel Press

Published in the United States of America by Cherry Lake Publishing
Ann Arbor, Michigan
www.cherrylakepublishing.com

Content Adviser: Stephen Ditchkoff, Professor of Wildlife Ecology and Management, Auburn University, Alabama
Reading Adviser: Marla Conn MS, Ed., Literacy specialist, Read-Ability, Inc.
Book Designer: Melinda Millward

Photo Credits: © Andaman/Shutterstock.com, cover, 1, 21; © Kitch Bain/Shutterstock.com, 5; ©Kasparart/Dreamstime.com, 6; ©NOAA/NMFS/SEFSC Pascagoula Laboratory; Collection of Brandi Noble, NOAA/NMFS/SEFSC/http://www.flickr.com/CC-BY-2.0, 6; © Nature Picture Library / Alamy Stock Photo, 7; © Norbert Wu/ Minden Pictures/Newscom, 8; © Moizhusein/Dreamstime.com, 10; © Artush/Shutterstock.com, 10; © Eric Isselee/Shutterstock.com, 10; © Suateracar/Dreamstime.com, 11; © Alta Oosthuizen/Shutterstock.com, 12; © SteveAllenPhoto/Thinkstock, 12; © Stephan Raats/Shutterstock.com, 12; © Jezbennett/Dreamstime.com, 13; © Mike Bauer/Shutterstock.com, 14; © Dai Mar Tamarack/Shutterstock.com, 14; © Marty Wakat/Shutterstock.com, 14, 15; © Dennis W Donohue/Shutterstock.com, 16; © Katherine McGovern/Shutterstock.com, 16; © aaltair/Shutterstock.com, 17; © Stuart G Porter/Shutterstock.com, 17; © Sainam51/Shutterstock.com, 18; © Moments_by_Mullineux/Thinkstock, 18; © FLPA / Alamy Stock Photo, 19; © Ewan Chesser/Shutterstock.com, 19; © Joze Maucec/Shutterstock.com, 20; © cbpix/Shutterstock.com, 20; © feathercollector/Shutterstock.com, 20; © Nastya81/Dreamstime.com, 22; © HUBERT YANN/iStockphoto, 24; © scubaluna/iStockphoto, 24; © Song Heming/Dreamstime.com, 24; © Orlandin/Dreamstime.com, 25; © Aneese/Thinkstock, 26; © Julian W/Shutterstock.com, 26; © Juniors Bildarchiv GmbH / Alamy Stock Photo, 27; © Frances van der Merwe/Shutterstock.com, 28; © inkwelldodo/Shutterstock.com, 28; © Andrey Pavlov/Thinkstock, 28; © Steven Ellingson/Shutterstock.com, 29; © Szasz-Fabian Jozsef/Shutterstock.com, 30; © 4loops/iStockphoto, 31

Graphic Element Credits: ©tukkki/Shutterstock.com, back cover, front cover, multiple interior pages; ©paprika/Shutterstock.com, back cover, front cover, multiple interior pages; ©Silhouette Lover/Shutterstock.com, multiple interior pages

45th Parallel Press is an imprint of Cherry Lake Publishing.

Library of Congress Cataloging-in-Publication Data

Names: Loh-Hagan, Virginia, author. | Loh-Hagan, Virginia. Wild wicked wonderful.
Title: Top 10 : partnerships / by Virginia Loh-Hagan.
Other titles: Top ten partnerships
Description: Ann Arbor, Michigan : Cherry Lake Publishing, [2017] | Series:
   Wild wicked wonderful | Includes index.
Identifiers: LCCN 2016029719| ISBN 9781634721394 (hardcover) | ISBN 9781634722711 (pbk.) |
   ISBN 9781634722056 (pdf) | ISBN 9781634723374 ebook)
Subjects: LCSH: Mutualism (Biology)—Juvenile literature. | Animal behavior—Juvenile literature. |
   Animals—Miscellanea—Juvenile literature.
Classification: LCC QH548.3 .L64 2017 | DDC 577.8/52—dc23
LC record available at https://lccn.loc.gov/2016029719

Printed in the United States of America
Corporate Graphics

About the Author

Dr. Virginia Loh-Hagan is an author, university professor, former classroom teacher, and curriculum designer. She lives in San Diego and has an extreme partnership with her very tall husband and very naughty dogs. To learn more about her, visit www.virginialoh.com.

TABLE OF CONTENTS

INTRODUCTION

Animals team up. They work together. They hunt together. They defend each other.

Animal partners need each other to survive. They depend on each other. They **benefit** from their partnership. Benefit means to get something good.

Some animals have extreme partnerships. They're nature's odd couples. Some animal partnerships are odder than others. These are the most exciting partnerships in the animal world!

Animal partners decide to collaborate instead of compete.

FEMALE AND MALE ANGLERFISH

Female and male anglerfish don't look the same. Females have a rod. The rod comes out of their forehead. It's like a fishing rod. It has millions of bacteria. The bacteria makes light. Females use it like a **lure**. They attract **prey**. Prey is food. They also use rods to attract male partners.

Females are **predators**. Predators are hunters. Females have big heads. They have long teeth. Their teeth look like fangs. They have a **flexible** stomach. They swallow prey twice their size.

Anglerfish are bony fish.
They live in icy blackness.

Males are 40 times smaller than females. They have tiny teeth. They don't have any guts. They don't have rods. They're weak.

They grab onto females. They bite into their skin. Then, their bodies break down. Their jaws become part of the females' skin. Their veins join with the females' veins. Males become bumps. They live on females' bodies. They depend on females for food.

Males become bigger when attached to females. They pay females back. They help the females have babies. Both benefit.

Did You Know...?

- Some animal partners evolve together. Evolve means to change over time. Animal partners adapt to the environment.

- Egrets don't just ride on hippos. They ride on the backs of other large animals. Partners include rhinos, elephants, and horses.

- Zebras also partner with oxpeckers. Oxpeckers are birds. They eat parasites off zebras. But they're not always helpful. Some oxpeckers pick open wounds on a zebra's back. This encourages more parasites to come. This creates more food for the oxpeckers.

- Male and female hornbills have an extreme partnership. Females use their own poop to make nests inside trees. They seal themselves inside. They make a tiny hole. Males hunt for food. They throw up the food and pass it through the hole.

Chapter two

ZEBRAS AND OSTRICHES

Zebras and ostriches roam together. Ostriches are the tallest birds. They're the biggest birds. They have the biggest eyes. They see far. They see from a high point. They see details very clearly. They're fast. But they can't zoom to top speed. They need a head start. They need zebras. Zebras smell very well. Together, they see and smell predators.

Zebras talk to each other. They warn others to run away. Ostriches know zebras' alarm call. They run away, too. Ostriches also alert others. They hiss or grunt. Both animals run when threatened. This confuses predators.

Zebras and ostriches live on savannas.
Savannas are warm grasslands.

Chapter three
CATTLE EGRETS AND HIPPOS

Adult hippos are dangerous. They charge. They attack. They run faster than humans. Their huge teeth crush bones. But baby hippos are **vulnerable**. They're unsafe.

Cattle egrets help. They serve as a lookout. They ride on hippos' backs. They can see a long way. They spot predators. They make a "kok-kok" sound. Then, hippos know to bunch up together. They protect their young.

Cattle egrets like when hippos travel together. This stirs

Cattle egrets also help hippos by eating harmful bugs off them.

up bugs. Cattle egrets can eat. They also get a free ride. This saves their energy. They can eat more.

Chapter four
GREEN SEA TURTLES AND YELLOW TANG FISH

Green sea turtles live 80 years. But they need to stay healthy. Yellow tang fish help. They travel in small groups. They swim in a coral reef. They eat **algae**. Algae are plants like seaweed. Yellow tang fish have tiny teeth. They bite off algae pieces. They eat all the time.

Algae grow on sea turtles' shells. This is dangerous. Algae can cause drag. This means sea turtles can't swim fast. Predators can catch slow sea turtles. Yellow tang fish eat the algae.

The coral reef can be like a cleaning station.

Both animals benefit. Yellow tang fish get a meal.
Sea turtles get their shells cleaned.

Chapter five

RED-BILLED HORNBILLS AND DWARF MONGOOSES

Red-billed hornbills follow dwarf mongooses. They watch them from the sky. They spot predators. They warn mongooses. They fly into trees. They call out. Mongooses scatter. They hide. Hornbills help mongooses hunt in peace.

Hornbills wake up mongooses. They wait in trees. They don't let mongooses sleep in. Hornbills call into the mongooses' **burrows**. Burrows are underground homes. Hornbills remind mongooses to get breakfast. Mongooses get up. They search. They dig. They hunt. They stir up bugs. Hornbills eat the bugs.

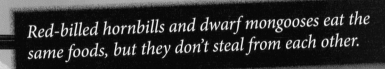

Red-billed hornbills and dwarf mongooses eat the same foods, but they don't steal from each other.

Chapter six

HONEYGUIDE BiRDS AND HONEY BADGERS

Honeyguide birds and honey badgers eat honey. Honeyguide birds can't open beehives. They need honey badgers to help them. Honey badgers need honeyguide birds to find the beehives.

Honeyguide birds fly from tree to tree. They find beehives. They call out. Honey badgers listen for the calls. They follow from the ground. Their short legs move fast. They climb trees. They tear open beehives. They use their sharp claws.

Angry bees attack. But honey badgers have thick skin. Bee stings don't hurt them. Honey badgers eat bees. They eat honey. Honeyguide birds eat leftovers. They eat the wax.

Honeyguide birds sound like the shaking of a box of matches.

19

Chapter seven

CLOWNFISH AND SEA ANEMONES

Sea anemones have **tentacles**. Tentacles are long arms. One tentacle sticks to a rock. Sea anemones never move. They wait for prey. They shoot out a tiny dart. The dart has poison. It stuns prey. Then, sea anemones move the prey into their mouths.

Clownfish need protection. They can't swim fast. They don't have sharp teeth. They partner with sea anemones. They hide in their tentacles. Clownfish rub against their tentacles. They rub sea anemone **mucus** on their skins. Mucus is like body snot. Sea anemones don't recognize

Sea anemones don't attack clownfish.

clownfish as food. Clownfish already have thick mucus on their skins. Their mucus pushes away anemone poison.

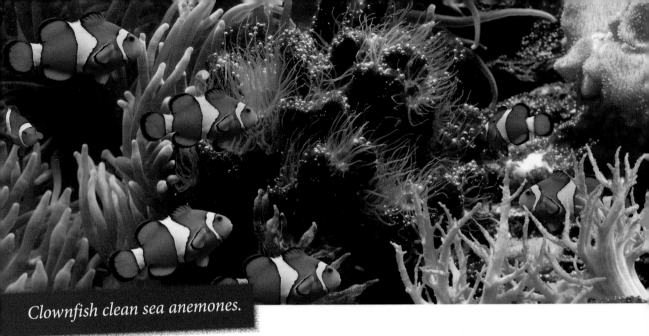

Clownfish clean sea anemones.

Clownfish protect sea anemones. Butterfly fish eat sea anemones. Poison doesn't affect them. Clownfish chase butterfly fish away.

Clownfish are bright. They lure prey. When prey comes, sea anemones trap it. Clownfish eat small animals and plants. Both animals leave crumbs. They eat each other's leftovers. They help each other eat.

Sea animals get oxygen by moving through water. But sea anemones don't move. Clownfish help. They stir up water. They swim in the tentacles. This brings more oxygen to sea anemones.

Humans Do What?!?

Humans and bacteria need each other. Bacteria need humans to eat. Humans need bacteria to stay healthy. Some people believe humans are washing away their good bacteria. Dave Whitlock is a chemical engineer. He graduated from Massachusetts Institute of Technology. He hasn't showered in over 12 years. (Sometimes he takes a sponge bath.) He wants to keep bacteria on his skin. He uses a special spray. The spray has live bacteria. He invented the spray. He sprays himself twice a day. Whitlock was inspired by a horse. The horse rolled on the ground to get a dirt bath. He said, "The only way that horses could evolve this behavior was if they had substantial evolutionary benefits from it." Humans are always learning from animals.

Chapter eight
GOBY FISH AND PISTOL SHRIMP

Goby fish and pistol shrimp share a home. Pistol shrimp live in burrows. They live under the ocean floor. Their claws push dirt and sand. They let goby fish live with them.

A burrow can cave in. It might bury goby fish. But goby fish aren't worried. Pistol shrimp will dig them out.

Goby fish protect pistol shrimp. They serve as pistol shrimp's eyes. Pistol shrimp can't see. Goby fish see

Pistol shrimp build burrows big enough for goby fish.

very well. Their fin touches the pistol shrimp's feelers. They dart to their burrow. This signals pistol shrimp to hide.

Chapter nine
NILE CROCODILES AND PLOVERS

Nile crocodiles are **carnivores**. They eat meat. They have strong jaws. They don't chew. They bite. They tear. They swallow. Meat gets stuck in their teeth. This can cause pain.

Egyptian plovers are birds. Their beaks are like toothpicks. They look for crocodiles with open mouths. They land in crocodiles' mouths. They pick out food scraps. They eat bugs off their skin. Then, they fly away. Both animals benefit. Plovers get food. Crocodiles get their teeth cleaned.

Egyptian plovers search for crocodiles around the Nile River.

Plovers also warn crocodiles. They scream and fly away.
Crocodiles quickly get underwater.

Chapter ten
ANTS AND APHiDS

Aphids are pests. They ruin crops. They eat the sugary fluid inside plants. They eat a lot. They poop a lot. Their poop is sweet. It's called **honeydew**.

Ants love honeydew. So, they herd aphids. Their feet release a drug. This slows aphids down. Ants turn aphids into slaves. Ants assign **shepherds**. Shepherds are caretakers. They protect aphids. They keep away predators. They kill predators' eggs. They ensure aphids eat enough. They carry aphids to new plants. They take care of aphids' eggs.

Ants stop disease from spreading to aphid herds. They get rid of the sick aphids.

Ants control the aphid population. Sometimes, they eat aphids, especially weak ones.

Ants take good care of aphids. But they don't want aphids to grow wings. They don't want aphids to fly away. Ants tear out aphid wings.

Ants milk aphids. They gently stroke the aphid's rear end. They use their feelers to do this. They force honeydew to come out. Some aphids can't poop. They need ants to milk them.

Both animals benefit. Ants feed on honeydew. They also use it to feed their babies. Aphids trade their freedom for protection.

When Animals Attack!

Coyotes and badgers don't get along. But they both eat squirrels and prairie dogs. So, sometimes they forget they're enemies. They work together to hunt. Badgers are great diggers. Coyotes are great runners. They combine their skills. Coyotes chase their prey. They tire out their prey. Prey hides underground. Then, badgers come to help. They dig the prey out of the burrow. Prey might try to escape the badgers, but coyotes chase them down. Some scientists think coyotes hunt more with badgers than with other coyotes. They've seen the same coyote-badger teams working together again and again. Whichever animal catches the prey gets to eat it. They don't share. But when coyotes and badgers attack as a team, they can't be stopped.

CONSIDER THIS!

TAKE A POSITION! Some scientists like to study animal relationships. What if scientists put different animals together to study them? Think about the advantages and disadvantages. Do you think this is the right thing to do? Argue your point with reasons and evidence.

SAY WHAT? Some animal partners are symbiotic. They need each other to survive. Mutual partnerships mean both animals benefit. Commensal partnerships mean one animal benefits and the other is unharmed. Partnerships with parasites are different. Parasites benefit. Their partners are harmed. Reread each animal partnership described in this book and explain the type of relationship.

THINK ABOUT IT! Animals and humans collaborate and compete. When is it important to collaborate? When is it important to compete? This book focused on animal collaborations. Think of ways in which animals compete instead of collaborate.

LEARN MORE!

- Cohn, Scotti, and Shennen Bersani (illustrator). *Animal Partners*. Mt. Pleasant, SC: Arbordale Publishing, 2015.
- Jenkins, Steve, and Robin Page. *How to Clean a Hippopotamus: A Look at Unusual Animal Partnerships*. Boston: HMH Books for Young Readers, 2010.
- *PBS Nature: Animal Odd Couples* (DVD), 2013.

GLOSSARY

algae (AL-jee) ocean plants like seaweed

benefit (BEN-uh-fit) to gain something positive or good

burrows (BUR-ohz) underground homes

carnivores (KAHR-nuh-vorz) meat eaters

flexible (FLEK-suh-buhl) easy to move

honeydew (HUHN-ee-doo) aphid poop that is really sweet

lure (LOOR) to draw in victims

mucus (MYOO-kuhs) body snot

predators (PRED-uh-turz) hunters

prey (PRAY) animals that are hunted for food

shepherds (SHEP-urdz) caretakers of a herd

tentacles (TEN-tuh-kuhlz) long flexible arm

vulnerable (VUHL-nur-uh-buhl) unsafe, open to danger

INDEX